Published By Robert Corbin

@ **Vincent Banker**

Go Vegan: Super-easy, Time-saving &

Weight Loss Recipes to Go Vegan for the

Right Reasons

All Right RESERVED

ISBN 978-87-94477-12-3

TABLE OF CONTENTS

Hearty Kale & Bulgur Salad 1

Blackberry & Arugula Salad 4

Quinta De Ravioli 6

Irresistible Garbanzo Beans Zest 9

Blueberry Waffles 12

Chickpea Omelette 14

Chapter Seven: Vegan Lunch Recipes 17

Loaded Veggie Tofu Pie 20

Philly Cheesesteak 22

Herb-Roasted Sweet Potato Wedges 24

Colleen's Yellow Split Pea Dal 26

Mary Mcdougall's Tunisian Sweet Potato Stew 28

Stuffed Eggplant 30

Tofu Scramble Southwest Style 32

Cauliflower Rice And Mushroom Risotto 34

White Bean & Chard Soup 36

Red Lentil-Spinach Stew 38

- Brut Rose Orange Pasta 40
- English Sparkling Tortilla 43
- French Toast 46
- Whole Bean Breakfast 48
- Snacks And Appetizers 50
- Spring Rolls 53
- Veggie Spring Rolls 56
- Steamed Eggplant And Mushrooms With Peanut Sauce 59
- Tofu Club Sandwich 61
- Italian–Style Spaghetti Squash With Tempeh 63
- Mexican Zucchini Casserole 65
- Dilled Chickpea Burger With Spicy Yogurt Sauce 67
- Instant Pot Black Beans And Rice 70
- One-Dish Baked Oatmeal Crisp 72
- Side Dish 74
- Moroccan Sweet Potato & Lentil Stew 77
- Turkish Split Pea Stew In An Instant Pot 79
- Beefless Stew 82

Tempeh & Kale Stir-Fry 85

Stir-Fried Bok Choy & Tofu 87

Polenta With Swiss Chard 89

Cotes De Pureed Cardamom Spinach 91

The Hedonist Cranberries Pasta 94

Zalze Green Lentils 97

Pumpkin Seed Alfredo Fussili 99

Cauliflower And Chickpea Stew With Couscous 103

Carrot Lemongrass & Cilantro Soup 105

Instant Pot Achari Aloo 107

Instant Pot Vegan Posole 110

Tuscany Style Vegetable Soup 112

Vegan Tempeh Blt Wrap 114

Millet And Eggplant Chickpea Stew 117

Roasted Vegetables And Lemon Vinaigrette 119

Coffele Fontina Broccoli 122

Creamy Shallots Le Corti 125

Greek Atma Pizzas 128

Zucchini Fritters 131

Oven Roasted Chickpeas 134

Banana Bread 136

Hearty Kale & Bulgur Salad

Ingredients

- 1 tablespoon tahini
- 1 tablespoon lemon juice
- 1 15.5-oz. can lentils, drained and rinsed
- ¼ cup toasted sunflower seeds
- ¼ teaspoon salt
- ½ cup bulgur wheat
- 1 bunch Tuscan (also called lacinato or "dinosaur") kale
- 1 tablespoon extra-virgin olive oil
- 1 tablespoon tamari (or low-sodium soy sauce)

Directions

1. Add the bulgur, 1 cup of water, and salt to a medium saucepan. Bring to a boil over medium-high heat. Cover, reduce heat, and simmer for 10–12 minutes or until tender. Drain excess liquid, and set aside.
2. In the meantime, wash and dry the kale leaves. Slice the kale leaves into bite-sized ribbons. The easiest way to do this is to stack the leaves on top of one another, and slice through several leaves at once. Discard any tough stem pieces.
3. Place the chopped kale into a large mixing bowl.
4. In a separate, small bowl, whisk together the olive oil, tamari, tahini, and lemon juice. Pour over the kale, and massage the dressing into the kale leaves, using your hands. Continue massaging until the kale has softened, about 1–2 minutes.

5. Add the bulgur, the drained lentils, and the sunflower seeds to the kale, and toss to combine.
6. Serve immediately, or chill to eat later. Stored covered in the refrigerator, it keeps for up to a week. Enjoy!

Blackberry & Arugula Salad

Ingredients

- 1 tablespoon extra virgin olive oil
- 1 tablespoon apple cider vinegar or lemon juice
- 2 tablespoons maple syrup
- 1 tablespoon Dijon mustard
- Salt and pepper to taste
- 4 cups arugula
- ½ pint blackberries
- 1 green apple, chopped
- ¼ cup chopped walnuts
- 2 oz. goat cheese, crumbled (optional)

Directions

1. Heat a small skillet over medium-high heat. Cook the walnuts, stirring frequently, until toasted and fragrant (about 3–5 minutes). Watch carefully so they do not burn. Set aside.
2. In a small bowl, whisk together the olive oil, vinegar or lemon juice, maple syrup, mustard, and salt and pepper.
3. In a large bowl, toss the dressing with the arugula.
4. Transfer the arugula to serving plates. Top with berries, apple, goat cheese (if using), and toasted walnuts. Enjoy!

Quinta de Ravioli

Ingredients:

- 2 tbsp. Greek yogurt
- 120g of ravioli
- 2 tbsp. coconut oil
- ½ tsp. sugar
- 1 tsp. salt
- 2 tbsp. fresh celery
- 1/2 a yellow onion
- 2 cloves of garlic
- 1 tsp. black pepper
- 3 ounces of Vacherin Mont d'Or
- 1-ounce of walnuts

Directions

1. Prepare the ravioli according to the package instructions, ensuring they are cooked to al dente perfection.
2. In a frying pan, heat some oil and add the sliced onion, grated carrot, and minced garlic. Sauté them until they become fragrant and slightly caramelized.
3. Sprinkle in the black pepper, salt, and sugar, and continue stirring the mixture over medium heat for about 10 minutes. This will allow the flavors to meld together beautifully.
4. Once the ravioli is cooked, drain it and add it directly to the frying pan with the sautéed vegetables. Toss everything together gently to combine.
5. Now it's time to enhance the dish with some delightful ingredients. Add the diced Vacherin Mont d'Or, chopped walnuts, and sliced celery to the pan. Allow the cheese to melt, creating a luscious, creamy coating for the ravioli.

6. To add a touch of tanginess and creaminess, stir in the Greek yogurt. Make sure it is warmed through before removing the pan from the heat.

Irresistible Garbanzo Beans Zest

Ingredients:

- ½ cup of cooked garbanzo beans
- 1 egg
- 2 tsp. lemon zest
- ½ cup of white wine
- 1 tsp. salt
- 2 tbsp. olive oil
- 2 cups of kale
- 1 tsp. ground black pepper

Directions

1. Heat one tbsp. olive oil in a skillet over medium heat. Add the kale, pepper, and salt to the skillet and stir until the kale wilts. This will take a few minutes.
2. Once the kale has wilted, add the lemon zest and garbanzo beans to the skillet. Using a fork

or a potato masher, gently smash the garbanzo beans to create a chunky mixture. Stir well to combine all the ingredients thoroughly.
3. Create a hole or indentation in the center of the mixture and drizzle the remaining tbsp. olive oil into the hole. Crack an egg into the hole as well, making sure to keep the yolk intact.
4. Cover the skillet with a lid and cook the mixture for about five minutes, or until the egg is cooked to your desired doneness. The egg yolk can be left runny or cooked through, depending on your preference.
5. Once the egg is cooked, transfer the garbanzo bean mixture to a plate. The dish is now ready to be served.
6. For added flavor, you can top the dish with a splash of white wine, such as Irresistible Leyda

Valley Sauvignon Blanc, which pairs well with the flavors of the dish.

Blueberry Waffles

Ingredients

- 1/3 Cup of unsweetened applesauce
- 1 and 1/2 cups of unsweetened almond milk
- 3 Tablespoons of pure maple syrup
- 2 Tablespoons of canola oil
- 1 Teaspoon of pure vanilla extract
- 1 and ½ cups of frozen blueberries
- 1 Cup of white whole wheat flour
- 1 Tablespoon of baking powder
- ½ Teaspoon of salt
- ¼ Teaspoon of ground allspice
- 1 Cup of quick cooking oats

Directions

1. Sift in the flour, the baking powder, the salt and the allspice in a deep mixing bowl.
2. Add the oats and pour the applesauce, the milk, the maple syrup, the oil and the vanilla in the centre
3. Keep stirring your ingredients until they are very- well incorporated
4. Set the batter aside for about 5 minutes
5. Add the blueberries and cook the batter in the waffle iron by pouring ½ cup of batter in the waffle iron
6. Don't forget to grease the iron with cooking spray or oil between the waffles

Chickpea Omelette

Ingredients

- ¼ Teaspoon of baking soda
- ⅛ Teaspoon and ¼ of sea salt
- ¼ of a red chopped onion
- 2 Minced garlic cloves
- ¼ Cup of chopped tomatoes
- ¼ Cup of small broccoli florets
- 1 Tablespoon of cilantro
- ¾ Cup and 1 tablespoon of unsweetened nondairy milk
- 2 Teaspoons of apple cider vinegar
- 2 Teaspoons of nutritional yeast
- ¼ Teaspoon of turmeric powder
- ¼ Teaspoon of garlic powder
- ¼ Teaspoon of onion powder

Directions

1. Whisk the chickpea batter in a bowl and make sure not to make the batter too thick
2. Set the batter aside for 10 minutes
3. Prepare a heated nonstick skillet and sauté the garlic and the red onion until it gets lightly browned.
4. Grease your heated skillet and add a drizzle of olive oil; then pour half of the prepared batter into your pan.
5. Add the onions, the broccoli and the garlic
6. Add the tomatoes right on top of each half of your batter
7. When the batter bubbles and becomes firm, flip it to the other side.
8. Cover the skillet and turn off your stove; then let it steam for about 5 minutes.
9. Garnish with the slices of the red onion, the tomato, the sliced avocado and the lime wedges.

10. Add 1 pinch of sea salt and add 1 pinch of pepper
11. Serve and enjoy your omelet!

Chapter Seven: Vegan Lunch Recipes

Ingredients:

- ½ cup raw sunflower seeds For balsamic dressing:
- ½ cup balsamic vinegar
- 4 tablespoons maple syrup
- 2 teaspoons Dijon mustard
- Juice of a lemon
- 4 tablespoons olive oil
- 1 teaspoon minced garlic
- Sea salt to taste
  Pepper to taste 1 bunch kale, de-stemmed and chopped into bite size pieces
- 1 small head red cabbage, chopped into bite size pieces
- 1 cup cooked black beans

- 2 large or 4 small roasted beets, chopped into bite size pieces
- 2 cups roasted Brussels sprouts
- 1 avocado, peeled, pitted, sliced
- 8 ounces spring mix
- 4 carrots, chopped
- 4 Portobello caps, chopped
- 1 cup red bell pepper, chopped

Directions

1. To make the dressing: Add all the ingredients of the dressing in a bowl. Whisk well. Add mushrooms into it and toss well.
2. Let it marinate in itovernight or at least for 3-4 hours.
   Transfer to a large serving bowl. Add kale, spring mix, cabbage,carrots, black beans,

beets and red pepper. Toss well. Refrigerate until use.

3. To serve: divide and serve the salad in individual serving bowls. Add Brussels sprouts, avocado and sunflower seeds on top and serve.

Loaded Veggie Tofu Pie

Ingredients:

- 2 cups carrots, chopped
- 2 cups celery leaves, chopped
- 2 medium tomatoes, sliced Black pepper powder to taste
- ¼ cup olive oil
- ¼ cup low sodium soy sauce
- 2 blocks extra firm tofu, crumbled
- 5 tablespoons Dijon mustard or to taste
- 4 cups fresh spinach, chopped
- 1 cup yellow or orange bell pepper, chopped
- 1 cup red bell pepper, chopped
- 8 spring onions, chopped
- ¼ cup nutritional yeast

Directions

1. Spray a baking dish with cooking spray. Add mustard, bell peppers, soy sauce, spinach, carrots, onions,tofu, and celery into the
2. baking dish. Mix well and press well on to the bottom of the dish.
3. Place tomato slices on top and sprinkle nutritional yeast.
4. Bake in a preheated oven at 400°F for 45-60 minutes.
5. Slice into wedges and serve.

Philly Cheesesteak

Ingredients:

- 2 teaspoons celery flakes
- Salt to taste
- Pepper to taste
- 4 vegan French rolls, halved lengthwise
- 1 medium yellow onions, sliced
- ½ teaspoon garlic powder
- ½ teaspoon onionpowder
- 2 packages (8 ounce each) seitan (vegan meat)

Directions

1. Place a large pan over medium heat. Add 4 tablespoons olive oil. When the oil is heated,

add green pepper, seitan and onion and sauté until the seitan is thoroughly heated.
2. Add onion powder, garlic powder, celery flakes, salt and pepperand mix well.
Place cheese slices on top.
3. Bake in a preheated oven at 375°F for 10 to 15 minutes or untilthe cheese melts.
Place another pan over medium heat. Add remaining oil. Cook theFrench rolls with the cut side facing down until brown and crisp.
4. Top rolls with the baked seitan filling and serve.

Herb-Roasted Sweet Potato Wedges

Ingredients

- Black Pepper
- juice from one lemon
- 1-3 organic sweet potatoes (depending how large of a batch you'd like to make)
- Herbs de Provence or Italian Seasoning blend

Directions

1. First, line a baking pan with either foil or choose a non-stick pan. Don't spray with non-stick spray. Or, alternately, you can use a large glass baking dish such as a casserole dish (no need to spray).
2. Preheat the oven to 425 degrees Fahrenheit.
3. Wash your potatoes and dry.
4. Chop each one in half lengthwise, then chop each half in half.

5. Repeat with each piece until you have 1 inch thick wedges.
6. Place on your pan and spread them out evenly.
7. Squeeze the juice of one lemon over the top (this helps the herbs stick to the potatoes better and brings out their sweet flavor).
8. Sprinkle your choice of seasoning across the top (even Mrs. Dash is good here too!).
9. Add the black pepper in however much you like (I like a lot.).
10. Roast in the oven on a rack that's placed in the middle oven the oven (not too high like a broiler pan and not on the bottom rack).
11. Let them roast for 45-50 minutes until golden brown on the outside. They'll be slightly crispy on the outside but still soft inside.
12. Remove, let cool for 10 minutes on the pan and serve. Or, let them cool for 30 minutes and refrigerate for later use.

Colleen's Yellow Split Pea Dal

Ingredients:

- 1 teaspoon ground cumin
- ½ teaspoon ground turmeric
- ¼ teaspoon chili powder
- 2 tablespoons tomato paste
- 1 cup yellow split peas, uncooked
- ¼ teaspoon salt (or to taste)
- Fresh cilantro or parsley, for garnish (optional)
- 3 cups plus 2 to 3 tablespoons water, for sautéing, divided
- 1 medium-size yellow onion, finely chopped
- 3 garlic cloves, pressed or minced
- 1 teaspoon finely minced fresh ginger
- 1 teaspoon curry powder

Directions:

1. Heat 2 to 3 tablespoons water in a 3-quart saucepan. Cook onion, garlic, and ginger until they start to soften, about 5 minutes. To prevent sticking, use more water.
2. Add curry powder, cumin, turmeric, and chili powder, and cook for 3 minutes, stirring frequently. Add more water, as necessary.
3. Add tomato paste, and cook, stirring, for a minute or so, thoroughly mixing paste with other ingredients.
4. Add 3 cups water and split peas, and stir to combine. Bring to a boil, then cover and simmer for 35 to 40 minutes, until split peas are soft and broken down.
5. Add more water, if necessary. Simmer, stirring frequently, until mixture is thick.
6. Add salt.
7. Top each bowl with fresh cilantro or parsley, if desired, and serve.

Mary Mcdougall's Tunisian Sweet Potato Stew

Ingredients:

- 5 cups peeled and chunked sweet potatoes or Garnet yams
- 2 14.5 ounce cans chopped tomatoes
- 2 14.5 ounce cans garbanzo beans, drained and rinsed
- 1 cup green beans, cut into 1 inch pieces
- 1 ½ cups vegetable broth
- ¼ cup natural peanut butter
- ¼ cup chopped cilantro
- 1/3 cup water
- 1 onion, chopped
- 2 jalapenos, seeded and finely chopped
- 2 teaspoons minced fresh ginger

- 1 teaspoon minced fresh garlic
- 2 teaspoons ground cumin
- ½ teaspoon ground cinnamon
- ¼ teaspoon crushed red pepper
- ¼ teaspoon ground coriander

Directions:

1. Place the water, onion, jalapenos, ginger and garlic in a large pot. Cook, stirring occasionally for 5 minutes.
2. Add cumin, cinnamon, red pepper and coriander. Cook and stir for 1 minute.
3. Add sweet potatoes or yams, tomatoes, garbanzo beans, green beans, vegetable broth and peanut butter. Bring to a boil, reduce heat and simmer for 30 minutes until sweet potatoes or yams are tender.
4. Stir in cilantro and let rest for 2 minutes.

Stuffed Eggplant

Ingredients:

- Parsley, fresh chop, three tablespoons to garnish
- Quinoa, cooked, two cups
- Red onion, one, diced
- Salt, one half teaspoon
- Soy yogurt, plain, one half cup
- Thyme, fresh chop, one tablespoon
- Black pepper, one teaspoon
- Eggplant, two medium-size cut in half
- Garlic, two cloves, minced
- Kale, two cups, chopped
- Lemon juice, one tablespoon
- Lemon zest, one tablespoon
- Mushrooms, button, one cup, thinly sliced

- Olive oil, three tablespoons divide

Directions

1. Heat the oven to 400. Use a spoon to scoop one-third of the flesh out of the eggplant and save it for some other use.
2. Use half of the olive oil to coat the eggplant halves and place them on a baking pan that is covered with foil or parchment paper with the inside facing up.
3. Use the rest of the olive oil to cook onions, mushrooms, garlic, kale, and quinoa for five minutes. Use lemon juice, lemon zest, pepper, salt, and thyme to season this mix. Use this mix to fill the eggplant halves and bake them for twenty minutes. Sprinkle with parsley and serve sides of yogurt for dipping.

Tofu Scramble Southwest Style

Ingredients:

Scramble

- Red onion, one fourth, thinly sliced
- Red pepper, one half, thinly sliced
- Tofu, firm, two cups
- Kale, two cups, chopped
- Olive oil, two tablespoons

Sauce

- Salt, one half teaspoon
- Turmeric, one quarter
- Water, just enough to thin ingredients
- Chili powder, one quarter teaspoon
- Cumin powder, one half teaspoons
- Garlic powder, one half teaspoon

Directions

1. Mix the spices in a bowl and add just enough water to stir them into a sauce-like consistency.
2. Cook the onion, red pepper, and kale for three to four minutes in the olive oil. Chop up the chunk of tofu into small pieces and add it to the veggie mix in the skillet.
3. Fry, stirring often, until the tofu is warmed and slightly brown, four to five minutes.

Cauliflower Rice and Mushroom Risotto

Ingredients:

- Onion, one small, well diced
- Parsley, fresh, two tablespoons, chopped
- Salt, one half teaspoon
- Shallot, one large, minced
- Soy yogurt, one cup
- Vegetable broth, two cups, divided
- Black pepper, one teaspoon
- Cauliflower, four cups, riced
- Garlic, minced, six cloves
- Mushrooms, button, one cup sliced thin
- Nutritional yeast, one half cup
- Olive oil, two tablespoons

Directions

1. Add the olive oil and the butter together in one pan and fry the shallot, onion, and garlic for five minutes. Pour in one cup of the vegetables broth and the mushrooms and cook for five more minutes.
2. Blend into this mix the other cup of vegetable broth and the riced cauliflower and cook for ten minutes while stirring often. Pour in the pepper, parsley, yogurt, salt, and the nutritional yeast and turn the heat under the pot to low.
3. Allow this mixture to simmer for ten to fifteen minutes or until the mix is thickened.
4. Nutrition info per serving: Calories 297, eight grams carbs, seven grams protein, twenty-six grams fat

White Bean & Chard Soup

Ingredients

- 1 bunch chard, chopped
- 2 carrots, peeled and chopped
- 4 cups vegetable broth
- Salt and pepper to taste 1 tablespoon extra virgin olive oil
- 1 yellow onion, chopped
- 2 cloves garlic, minced
- 1 15-oz. can white beans, drained and rinsed

Directions

1. In a large saucepan, sauté the onions in the olive oil over medium-high heat. Cook until onions are tender, about 5 minutes. Stir in the garlic.
2. Add the white beans, carrots, and broth to the pot. Cover and bring to a boil. Reduce heat to

medium-low and simmer for 10 minutes, until carrots are tender.

3. Add the chard to the pot and cook for an additional 5 minutes.
4. Remove the pot from the heat, and use a potato masher or immersion blender to mash the beans. If it seems too thick, add water or more broth. Taste, and season with salt and pepper, if desired. Enjoy!

Red Lentil-Spinach Stew

Ingredients

- 4 cups water
- 1 teaspoon cumin
- ½ teaspoon cayenne pepper (or to taste)
- 2 cups baby spinach
- Salt and pepper to taste 2 tablespoons coconut oil
- ½ yellow onion, chopped
- 2 cloves garlic, minced
- ½ pound red lentils (dried)
- 1 15.5-oz. can diced tomatoes

Directions

1. In a large saucepan, sauté the onions in the coconut oil over medium-high heat. Cook until onions are tender, about 5 minutes. Stir in the garlic.

2. Add the lentils and water to the pot. Cover and bring to a boil. Reduce heat to medium-low and simmer for 10 minutes, until lentils are tender.
3. Stir in the tomatoes, spices, and spinach, and cook for an additional 5 minutes.
4. Taste, and season with salt and pepper, if desired. Enjoy!

Brut Rose Orange Pasta

Ingredients:

- 1/4 cup of mashed bananas
- 2 tbsp. coconut oil
- 2 tbsp. cornflakes
- 1 tsp. salt
- 1/4 cup of toasted almonds
- 2 cloves of garlic
- 8-ounces of quinoa pasta, uncooked
- 2 tbsp. orange juice
- 1 cup of Grana Padano
- 1 tsp. ground black pepper
- 8 fresh basil leaves

Directions

1. Cook the pasta according to the package Directionsuntil it reaches the desired tenderness. Drain and set aside.
2. In a nonstick skillet, heat oil over medium heat. Add minced garlic and mashed bananas to the skillet. Stir and sauté until the garlic becomes fragrant and the bananas soften slightly.
3. Add cornflakes to the skillet and continue stirring until they turn golden brown and crispy.
4. In a separate bowl, whisk together orange juice and cornflour until well combined. Pour the mixture into the skillet with the garlic, bananas, and cornflakes. Stir well to combine all the ingredients.
5. Pour the sauce over the cooked pasta and toss until the pasta is evenly coated.
6. Season the pasta with salt and pepper to taste. Add toasted almonds, fresh basil leaves,

and grated Grana Padano cheese. Toss the pasta gently to incorporate all the ingredients.
7. Serve the Brut Rosé Orange Pasta warm, and garnish with additional basil leaves and grated Grana Padano, if desired.

English Sparkling Tortilla

Ingredients:

- 2 tbsp. capers
- 4 tbsp. fresh parsley chopped
- 2 tortillas
- 4 eggs
- 28-ounces of chopped tomatoes
- 1 red bell pepper diced
- ½ tbsp. smoked paprika
- 30g of Ricotta cheese
- 1 tbsp. olive oil
- 200g of chickpeas
- 2 tsp. garlic powder
- 1 medium onion diced
- 1 tsp. cayenne pepper

- 1 tsp. fennel seeds

Directions

1. Heat oil in a pan and add garlic powder, chopped bell pepper, and onion. Sauté them for about 5 minutes until they start to soften and become aromatic.
2. Add tomatoes to the pan and continue cooking. Then, add chickpeas, paprika, fennel seeds, and cayenne pepper to the mixture. Stir everything together to form a flavorful sauce base. Let it cook for another 5 minutes to allow the flavors to meld.
3. Create wells in the sauce and crack an egg into each well. This will allow the eggs to cook directly in the sauce, giving the tortilla its characteristic texture. Make sure the heat is at a medium-low setting to cook the egg whites gently.

4. Cook the tortilla for about 10 minutes, or until the egg whites are fully set. You can cover the pan with a lid to help the eggs cook evenly.
5. Once cooked, top the tortilla with dollops of ricotta cheese, capers, and fresh parsley. These additions will provide creamy, tangy, and herbaceous flavors to complement the dish.

French toast

Ingredients:

- 1 Tablespoon of sugar
- 1 Tablespoon of nutritional yeast
- 1 Teaspoon of cinnamon
- 6 Slices of bread
- 1 Cup of vanilla-flavored soymilk
- 2 Tablespoons of flour

Directions

1. Combine the ingredients altogether except for the slices of bread
2. Dip each of the bread pieces in your mixture and cook it into a skillet until it becomes golden
3. Repeat the same process until you finish with all the slices of bread

4. Serve and enjoy your delicious toasted bread

Whole Bean Breakfast

Ingredients:

- 1 Tablespoon of Kosher salt
- 3 Tablespoons of Copious extra-virgin olive oil
- 1 and ½ lemons
- Parsley leaves
- 1 Pinch of freshly ground black pepper
- 1 lb of dried dark brown marrowfat peas
- 1 Cup of cooked garbanzo beans
- 4 Finely minced garlic cloves garlic
- 1 Teaspoon of cumin

Directions:

1. Start by rinsing the beans and clean your beans of any extra material.
2. Cover the beans with water and soak it overnight.

3. Drain the water and add 2 to 3 cups of fresh water to the beans.
4. Boil the beans for about 40 minutes, and cook it until it becomes tender; pour more water if you need more
5. Drain your cooked beans, but don't spill the cooking liquid; you will use it later as a broth
6. Toss your marrowfat peas with the chickpeas
7. Add the garlic, the cumin, 1 pinch of kosher salt and around 2 tbsp. of olive oil.
8. Spoon your beans into bowls and pour a little bit of hot broth over the top of the beans. You can mash your beans and add more olive oil.
9. Garnish the bans with lemon juice and wedges, parsley, oregano and 1 pinch of ground black pepper.
10. Serve your beans and enjoy its delicious taste!

Snacks and Appetizers

Ingredients:

- 1 Pinch of Kosher salt
- ½ Cup of cold water
- 2Tbsp of rice vinegar
- 1 Head of cauliflower broken into florets
- 1 Sweet and Spicy Chilli Sauce
- 5 Sliced scallions
- 2 Quarts of peanut oil or vegetable oil
- ½ Cup of cornstarch
- ½ Cup of all purpose flour
- ½ Teaspoon of baking powder
- ½ Cup of toasted sesame seeds
- 1/3 Cup of unsweetened coconut flakes

Directions:

1. Preheat your oil to about 350°F into a wok or in a deep fryer.
2. Combine the cornstarch, the flour, the baking powder, 2 teaspoons of kosher salt
3. Add the sesame seeds and the coconut into a bowl and then whisk it until it becomes homogenous.
4. Add the water and the rice vinegar and mix until you get a smooth batter
5. Add 2 tablespoons of water if the batter becomes too thick.
6. Add the cauliflower to the batter and lift each piece and allow the batter to drip off it.
7. Lower the heat and repeat dip the rest of your ingredients into the prepared batter
8. Fry the cauliflower until it becomes golden brown and crispy.

9. Transfer the fried cauliflower to a paper towel serving platter and sprinkle with scallions and sesame.
10. Serve and enjoy your fried cauliflower!

Spring Rolls

Ingredients:

- 1 Cup of thinly sliced kale
- 1 Cup of thinly sliced Napa cabbage
- 1 Diced scallion
- ½ Teaspoon of salt
- ¼ Cup of low sodium soy sauce
- 1 Tablespoon of rice vinegar
- 1 Teaspoon of sesame oil
- 11 Spring roll wrappers
- 4 Tablespoons of coconut oil
- 1 Small finely diced yellow onion
- 1 Minced garlic clove
- 1 Teaspoon of freshly grated ginger
- 1 Large grated carrot

- 8 Diced shiitake mushrooms

Directions:

1. Heat about 1 tablespoon of oil in a large wok over a medium heat.
2. Add your onions, sauté for about 2 minutes.
3. Add the ginger, the garlic, the carrots and the mushrooms; then sauté it for about 3 minutes. Add the kale, the cabbage, the scallions and the salt and sauté your ingredients for about 3 additional minutes
4. In a small deep bowl, combine together the rice vinegar; pour in the soy sauce and the sesame oil
5. Add your ingredients to the skillet and stir; let it on fire for 3 minutes
6. Remove your ingredients from the heat and set it aside to cool
7. Put 1 spring roll wrapper above a flat hard surface with its corner facing you, so that it makes a shape of a diamond.

8. Put 2 tablespoons of your prepared filling into along the middle of your wrapper. Fold the corners of the roll and roll it to the centre
9. Brush the roll with a little bit of water right on top of its corner and roll it like your roll burritos
10. Heat the remaining oil into a wok over a medium heat. Put your spring rolls into a pan and make sure that you have the room to roll it. Cook the spring rolls for 4 minutes or you can bake it in the oven at about 425° F for about 25 minutes
11. Serve and enjoy your rolls!

Veggie Spring Rolls

Ingredients:

For Spring Rolls:

- 1 small beet, halved, thinly sliced
- 1 small ripe avocado, peeled, thinly sliced
- 1 small radish, peeled, thinly sliced
- 1 cup red cabbage, finely chopped
- 1 cup carrot, grated
- 4 rice paper wrappers
- 4large fresh mint leaves
- 4 large fresh basil For peanut sauce:
- 2 tablespoons natural peanut butter
- 1 tablespoon water
- 2 teaspoons pure maple syrup
- A pinch crushed red pepper

- 1 tablespoon tamari or soy sauce
- 1 teaspoon rice vinegar
- 1 clove garlic, minced

Directions

1. Take a shallow dish and pour very hot water in it. Dip one rice wrapper in it and let it soak for about 30 seconds or until soft. Gently remove from the bowl and shake to drop off excess water. Place on your cutting board.
2. Repeat with the remaining wrappers. Divide and place beets, avocado and radish next to each other (in the same order given) on the center of the wrappers.
3. Place carrots on top of the beets and cabbage on top of theavocado and radish.
   Place a basil leaf on the carrot and a mint leaf on the cabbage.Fold over the filling and wrap tightly like a burrito. Cut into 2 halves. Serve with the peanut sauce.

4. Mix together all the ingredients of the sauce into a bowl until smooth and well combined.

Steamed Eggplant and Mushrooms with Peanut Sauce

Ingredients:

- 3 Japanese eggplants sliced into 1-inch-thick rounds
- 1 ½ tablespoons smooth peanut butter
- 1 tablespoon soy sauce
- 1 tablespoon light brown sugar
- Coarse salt to taste
- Cooked rice, to serve (optional)
- ½ pound shiitake mushrooms, stems discarded, caps halved
- 1 ½ tablespoons rice vinegar
- 1 tablespoon, peeled, fresh ginger, finely grated

- 2 scallions, cut into 2-inch lengths, thinly sliced lengthwise

Directions

1. Place a pot over medium heat. Pour enough water to cover an inch from the bottom of the pot. Add eggplant and mushrooms. Steam the eggplant and mushrooms for a few minutes until tender. Transfer to a bowl.
2. Add peanut butter and vinegar into a small bowl and whisk untilsmooth.
    Add rest of the ingredients and whisk well. Add this to the bowlof eggplants. Add scallions and toss. Serve hot with rice.

Tofu Club Sandwich

Ingredients:

- 2 packages tofu, cut into slices of 4-5 mm
- Few lettuce leaves
- 1 cup onion or shallots, sliced
- 2 tomatoes, sliced
- 1 avocado, peeled, pitted, sliced
- 2 teaspoons dried rosemary
- Tahini, as required
- Salt to taste
- Pepper to taste
- Few fresh basil leaves
- 4 cloves garlic, minced

- 8 -12 slices bread of your choice, toasted
  Cooking spray

Directions

1. Place a large nonstick pan over medium heat. Spray with cooking spray. Add garlic, onions and rosemary. Sauté until onions are translucent.
2. Add tofu slices and cook until golden brown. Flip sides and cookthe other side too.
3. Apply tahini on the bread slices. Place lettuce, mustard, avocado,tomato and tofu in the order mentioned on half the bread slices. Top with the remaining bread slices.
4. Cut each club sandwich into 2 triangles and serve.

Italian–Style Spaghetti Squash with Tempeh

Ingredients:

- 24 ounces tempeh, cut into small cubes
  ½ cup mirin

- 2 spaghetti squashes (2.5 pounds each), halved lengthwise, deseeded

- 2 jars (25 ounces each) pasta sauce

- 2 cups packed baby spinach

- 4 tablespoons tamari

- 4 cloves garlic, finely chopped

- 2 tablespoons canola oil

- 4 cups broccoli, cut into small florets

Directions

1. Place the squash with its cut side facing down in a large baking dish. Add 1-cup water.

2. Bake in a preheated oven at 375°F for 30-45 minutes or until thesquash is tender.

3. Meanwhile, add tempeh, tamari, garlic and mirin into a bowl.Toss well and set aside for 30 minutes. Drain.

4. Place a large skillet over medium high heat. Add tempeh and cookuntil golden brown. Stir once in a while. Remove on to a plate and keep warm.

5. 5. 6 minutes until crisp as well as tender.

6. Add spinach and stir. Remove from heat.

7. When the squash is done, remove from the oven and keep it withits cut side facing up. Let it cool.

8. Shred the squash with a pair of forks and place on a large servingplatter. Pour hot broccoli and sauce over it. Place tempeh on top and serve.

Mexican Zucchini Casserole

Ingredients:

- 2 tablespoons fresh cilantro, chopped
- 2 tablespoons extra virgin olive oil
- 4 tablespoons nutritional yeast + extra for topping ½ teaspoon salt

  ½ teaspoon pepper powder
- 2 ½ tablespoons flaxseed meal
- 2 cups zucchini, shredded
- 2 jalapeño peppers, deseeded, finely chopped 1 small onion, chopped

  ¾ cup Bisquick baking mix
- 2.5 ounces water

Directions

1. To make egg substitute: Add flaxseed meal and water into a bowl and mix well. Place in the refrigerator for 15-20 minutes. 2 Add zucchini, onions, cilantro and jalapeño into a bowl and mix well.
2. Add oil into egg substitute. Mix well and pour over the zucchini mixture. Mix until well combined.
3. Add Bisquick mix, salt, pepper, and nutritional yeast and stir again. Transfer this mixture into a parchment paper lined or greased baking dish.

Dilled Chickpea Burger with Spicy Yogurt Sauce

Ingredients:

- ounces canned or cooked chickpeas, rinsed, drained ¼ cup shallots, minced
- 2 tablespoons fresh dill, minced
- 1-2 tablespoon dry bread crumbs
- 1 tablespoon tahini
- 1 tablespoon lemon juice
- Salt to taste
- Pepper powder to taste
- ¼ teaspoon ground cumin
- 2 tablespoons vegetable oil
- 3 pita pockets For the sauce:
- ½ cup vegan yogurt

- 1 clove garlic, peeled, minced
- ¼ teaspoon curry powder
- ¼ teaspoon cayenne powder
- A large pinch salt

Directions

1. Add half the chickpeas, tahini, lemon juice, salt, pepper, and cumin to the food processor bowl and process until smooth in texture.
2. Add remaining half chickpeas into a bowl and mash lightly. Addshallots, dill, lemon juice and bread crumbs. Add the processed chickpea mixture into it. Mix well.
3. Divide the mixture into 3 equal portions and shape into patties.
   Place a nonstick skillet over medium heat and add oil.
4. When theoil is heated, place the burgers and cook on both the sides until golden brown.

Stuff the burger in the pita pockets and serve with sauce.

5. To make the sauce: Add all the ingredients to a bowl and whiskthoroughly.

Instant Pot Black Beans and Rice

Ingredients

- 9 cups water
- 1 teaspoon salt
- 1-2 limes (optional)
- Avocado (optional)
- 1 cup diced onion
- 4 cloves of garlic, crushed and minced
- 2 cups brown rice
- 2 cups dry black beans

Directions

1. Dump diced onion and garlic into the Instant Pot liner.
2. Add the brown rice and black beans.
3. Pour the water into the pot liner and add the salt.
4. Secure the lid with the vent sealed.

5. Select Manual, using the arrows decrease time to 28 minutes.
6. Once the time is up you can press cancel or unplug the Instant Pot. Allow the pressure to naturally release. (I let it set for 20 minutes before opening the lid.)
7. Scoop into bowls and squeeze a lime wedge over bowl and stir. Then add a few slices of avocado for garnish.

Dish Baked Oatmeal Crisp

Ingredients:

- No oil/unsweetened non-dairy milk, as required (you can also do half water/half non-dairy milk if you like...I used unsweetened vanilla almond milk only)
- Frozen fruit (enough to layer a baking dish)
- Quick-cooking oats (enough to cover the frozen fruit by one inch in the baking dish)

Directions:

1. Pre-heat oven to 350 degrees F.
2. In a baking dish layer the following:
3. 1 layer of frozen fruit
4. 1 layer of quick-cooking oats (enough to cover the frozen fruit by one inch in the baking dish)
5. Next, pour non-dairy milk over the oats so that the oats are well covered.
6. Cover the baking dish with aluminum foil so that nothing overflows into the oven.

7. Bake in the oven at 350 degrees F. for about 35 minutes or until the non-dairy milk has absorbed into the oats (there shouldn't be any liquid). Enjoy!!

Side Dish

Ingredients

- ½ teaspoon dried oregano
- ½ teaspoon garlic powder
- 1 teaspoon kosher salt
- ¼ teaspoon pepper
- 3 tablespoons olive oil
- ½ cup water
- 2 pounds baby yukon golds and red potatoes, about 1 to 1 ½ inches
- ½ teaspoon dried rosemary
- ½ teaspoon dried thyme
- ½ teaspoon dried marjoram

Directions

1. Wash the potatoes and pat dry.

2. In a small bowl, combine rosemary, thyme, marjoram, oregano, garlic powder, salt, and pepper.
3. PRESS the SAUTE mode button on the Instant Pot. When HOT appears on the display, add oil and heat with the Instant Pot lid open.
4. Add potatoes in batches and arrange in a single layer.
5. Cook, rolling the potatoes on all sides, for about 5 to 6 minutes or until lightly browned and crisp. Using a fork, pierce the middle of each potato. Alternatively, pan-fry potatoes in a skillet over medium heat until lightly browned and transfer to Instant Pot.
6. Toss in herb seasonings. Add water/stock.
7. Press KEEP WARM/CANCEL button. Close and lock the lid, making sure the floating valve is set on SEALING. Press the manual button, use the plus and minus buttons to adjust the cooking time to 7 minutes.

8. Once done, use quick release by pressing CANCEL and then turning the steam floating valve on the lid to VENTING position.
9. Open lid and transfer potatoes to serving platter. Serve hot.

Moroccan Sweet Potato & Lentil Stew

Ingredients:

- 1 stalk celery, chopped
- 1 c green or brown lentils
- ½ c red lentils
- 2 cups vegetable broth
- ¼ c raisins
- 1 can diced tomatoes
- Diced greens (optional)
- 1 lg onion, diced
- 3 cloves garlic, minced
- Moroccan spice blend (below)
- 1 sweet potato, peeled and cut into 1? cubes
- 2 carrots, peeled and diced

Directions

1. Sauté onions for 2-3 minutes, adding broth or water in small amounts as needed so they don't stick. Add garlic and cook for another minute. Add ½ of the spices, sweet potatoes, carrots, celery, and raisins. Cook for another minute or two. Stir in lentils and broth. Cover and set for manual, 10 minutes pressure. Turn off when done and allow pressure to come down naturally.
2. Once pressure is released, take off lid, press sauté, and stir in tomatoes and the other half of the spices. Cook for 5 minutes, stirring often. Taste and adjust seasonings. Turn off and stir in greens just before serving. Delicious served over quinoa!

Turkish Split Pea Stew In An Instant Pot

Ingredients

- ½ teaspoon salt
- ¼ teaspoon cinnamon powder
- ¼ teaspoon chili powder or cayenne pepper
- 2 cups split yellow peas (rinsed well)
- ½ cup chopped tinned tomatoes
- Juice of ½ lemon
- 1.75 L vegetable stock (I used 7 x 250 ml cups + 3 vegetable stock cubes)
- To serve: chopped chives or scallions, extra lemon and yoghurt (optional)
- 1½ tablespoons olive oil
- 1 medium white onion, diced
- 1 medium carrot, diced into small cubes
- 1 celery stick, diced into cubes

- 4-5 cloves garlic, diced finely
- 1 bay leaf
- 1 teaspoon paprika powder
- 1½ teaspoons cumin powder

Directions

1. Press the Sauté key on the Instant Pot (it should say Normal, 30 mins). Add the olive oil, onion, carrot and celery and cook for 4 minutes, stirring a few times.

2. Add the rest of the ingredients and stir. Cancel the Sauté function by pressing Keep Warm/Cancel button.

3. Place and lock the lid, make sure the steam releasing handle is pointing to Sealing. Press Manual (High Pressure) and adjust to 10 minutes. After 3 beeps the pressure cooker will start going.

4. Once the timer goes off, allow the pressure to release for 4-5 minutes and then use the quick release method before opening the lid.

5. Serve with chopped chives or scallions and extra lemon on the side. A dollop of full-fat natural yoghurt or coconut yoghurt (or other vegan option) is gorgeous stirred in.

Beefless Stew

Ingredients

- 2 pounds white potatoes, peeled and cut into ¾-inch chunks (about 6 cups)
- ? cup tomato paste (half of a 6-ounce can)
- 1 tablespoon dried Italian herb seasoning
- 1 tablespoon paprika
- 2 teaspoons finely chopped fresh rosemary
- 1½ cups cooked peas (if frozen, rinse under warm water)
- ½ cup fresh parsley, chopped
- 1½ large yellow or white onions, chopped into ¾-inch pieces (about 3 cups)
- 3 medium carrots, sliced lengthwise and cut into ¾-inch pieces (about 2¼ cups)
- 3 ribs celery, cut into ¾-inch pieces (about 1 cup)

- 2 medium portabella mushrooms, cut into ¾-inch pieces (about 4 cups)
- 1½ tablespoon finely chopped garlic (about 6 medium cloves)
- 5 cups water

Directions

1. Heat 1 tablespoon of water in a soup pot over medium-high heat. When the water starts to sputter, add the onions, carrots, and celery, and and cook, stirring frequently, for about 8 minutes, adding water as needed.
2. Stir in the mushrooms and garlic, and continue to cook while stirring for 5 minutes more, adding water as needed.
3. Add the 5 cups of water, potatoes, tomato paste, Italian seasoning, and paprika, and bring to a boil, uncovered. Reduce the heat to medium-low and stir in the rosemary. Cover and cook for 25 to 30 minutes, stirring

occasionally, or until the carrots and potatoes are very tender.
4. Add the peas and cook for 5 minutes more.
5. Place 2 cups of the stew (broth and vegetables) into a blender, and blend just briefly. Stir the mixture back into the pot to thicken the stew. Stir in the parsley.

Tempeh & Kale Stir-fry

Ingredients

- 1 8-oz. package of tempeh, cut into cubes
- 1 8-oz. package of sliced mushrooms
- 1 yellow onion, sliced
- 1 bunch kale, shredded
- 1 teaspoon sesame oil
- 2 tablespoons sesame seeds
- 2 tablespoons tamari (or soy sauce)
- 1 tablespoon rice wine vinegar
- 1 clove garlic, minced
- 1 tablespoon ginger, minced
- 1 tablespoon coconut oil

Directions

1. In a medium bowl, stir together the tamari, vinegar, garlic, and ginger.

2. Add tempeh and stir until all pieces are coated. Let tempeh marinate for at least 5 minutes.
3. Heat coconut oil in a large skillet over medium-high heat. Add onion, tempeh, and mushrooms, and sauté for 10 minutes.
4. Lower heat to medium, add kale and sesame oil, and stir until kale is wilted.
5. Sprinkle with sesame seeds and serve.Enjoy!

Stir-fried Bok Choy & Tofu

Ingredients

- 1 bunch bok choy, stems chopped
- 1 5-oz. can sliced bamboo shoots, drained
- 1 cup bean sprouts
- 1 package extra-firm tofu, cut into 1-inch cubes
- 1/4 teaspoon dried crushed red pepper
- 2 tablespoons tamari (or soy sauce)
- 1 tablespoon rice wine vinegar
- 1 clove garlic, minced
- 1 tablespoon ginger, minced
- 1 tablespoon coconut oil
- ½ yellow onion, sliced

Directions

1. In a small bowl, stir together the tamari, vinegar, garlic, and ginger.
2. Heat coconut oil until very hot in a large wok or skillet over high heat. Add onion and bok choy and stir-fry until just wilted, about 2 minutes. Add in bamboo shoots and bean sprouts and stir-fry about 1 minute.
3. Add tofu and stir-fry until tofu is heated through, about 2 minutes. Pour over tamari mixture and cook until liquid boils and thickens, about 1 minute.
4. Sprinkle with crushed red pepper and serve. Enjoy!

Polenta with Swiss Chard

Ingredients

- 1 15.5-oz. can diced tomatoes
- 1 bunch Swiss chard, chopped
- 1 teaspoon dried basil
- Salt and pepper to taste
- 2 tablespoons olive oil, divided
- 1 tube pre-cooked polenta
- 2 cloves garlic, minced
- 1 15.5-oz. can cannellini beans, drained and rinsed

Directions

1. In a large nonstick skillet, heat 1 tablespoon of olive oil over medium-low heat. Remove polenta from package and slice into 8 slices. Cook for 5 minutes on one side, then flip and cook for another 5 minutes.

2. In a separate skillet, heat 1 tablespoon of olive oil over medium heat. Add the garlic, tomatoes, basil, and beans and cook for about 2 minutes.
3. Stir the Swiss chard into the pan with the beans. Stir until the chard is tender, about 3 minutes. Taste, and season with salt and pepper, if desired.
4. To serve, place polenta on plates and top with the chard mixture. Enjoy!

Cotes de Pureed Cardamom Spinach

Ingredients:

- 2 tbsp. oil
- 12 ounces of mixed stir fry vegetables
- 3 cloves of garlic
- 14 ounces of cooked spinach
- 1/2 mild red chili
- 5-ounces of tofu
- 1/2 tsp. puréed cardamom
- 1 tsp. black pepper
- 4 tbsp. soy sauce

Directions

1. Heat a tbsp. oil in a pan or wok over medium heat. Add the onions, carrots, and broccoli. Stir fry for a few minutes until they start to soften.

2. Add the snow peas, bean sprouts, and leafy greens to the pan. Continue cooking and stirring for a few more minutes until the vegetables are slightly tender.
3. Sprinkle in the ginger, garlic powder, and soy sauce. Stir to coat the vegetables with the flavorful seasonings. Cook for another minute or two to allow the flavors to meld together.
4. In a separate pan, cook the tofu in the remaining oil for about 10 minutes until it is lightly browned and heated through. Add the cooked tofu to the vegetables and stir to combine.
5. Add the minced garlic, chili (optional for spice), ground cardamom, black pepper, and soy sauce to the pan. Stir well to evenly distribute the spices throughout the dish.
6. Finally, add the spinach to the pan and cook over medium heat. Stir occasionally until the spinach wilts and is fully cooked.

7. Once everything is cooked and well combined, remove from heat and serve hot.

The Hedonist Cranberries Pasta

Ingredients:

- 1 tsp. salt
- 6-ounces of spaghetti
- ¼ tsp. garlic powder
- 1 tbsp. lemon juice
- 6 tbsp. fresh dill
- 3 tbsp. olive oil
- 1 tsp. black pepper
- 5 spring onions
- 2 ounces of dried cranberries
- 3 ounces of Mascarpone cheese

Directions

1. Cook the spaghetti according to the package instructions. Drain and set aside.

2. In a mini food processor, combine the dill and garlic powder. Process until they are finely chopped.
3. Add salt, black pepper, lemon juice, and olive oil to the processor. Process until the ingredients form a paste-like consistency.
4. In a large skillet or pan, heat a small amount of olive oil over low heat. Add the cooked spaghetti and the cranberry paste mixture from the food processor.
5. Stir in the sliced spring onions, crumbled cheese, and your choice of dressing. Continue cooking over low heat for about two minutes, stirring occasionally until the cheese has melted and the ingredients are well combined.
6. Once the cheese has melted and the pasta is coated with the sauce, remove from heat.

7. Serve the Hedonist Cranberries Pasta immediately, garnished with additional fresh dill if desired.

Zalze Green lentils

Ingredients:

- 4 large pieces of sun-dried tomato
- 1/2 tsp. smoked paprika
- 1 tsp. salt
- 2 tbsp. fresh basil
- 3 tbsp. sour cream
- 1 cup of cooked green lentils
- 1 tsp. black pepper
- 8-ounces of spaghetti
- 1 cup of grated Parmesan cheese

Directions

1. Cook the spaghetti according to the package instructions. Once cooked, drain the water and set the pasta aside.

2. In a large pan, add the cooked spaghetti and mix in the grated cheese and sour cream. Stir well until the cheese is melted and the sour cream coats the pasta evenly.
3. Place the pan on low heat and add the smoked paprika, green lentils, and tomatoes. Stir to combine all the ingredients.
4. Season the mixture with salt and black pepper according to your taste. Continue stirring until a silky sauce forms and the lentils are heated through.
5. Once the sauce has reached the desired consistency and the lentils are tender, remove the pan from heat.
6. Serve the Zaize Green Lentils with fresh basil leaves for added flavor and garnish.

Pumpkin Seed Alfredo Fussili

Ingredients:

- 14-16 ounces uncooked fussili, cook according to Directionson the package
  For pumpkin seed Alfredo:
- 1 cup onions, chopped
- ½ cup raw pumpkin seeds
- 6 tablespoons nutritional yeast
- ½ teaspoon dried basil or oregano
- ½ teaspoon dried thyme
- 1 cup water
- 6 cloves garlic
- 4 tablespoons lemon juice
- 1 cup water, divided
- 1 teaspoon white vinegar

- Salt to taste
- ½ teaspoon red pepper flakes or to taste
- 2 cups nondairy milk like almond milk, coconut milk etc. Pepper powder to taste 2 tablespoons whole wheat flour
- 4 teaspoons extra virgin olive oil
- 2 teaspoons vegetable oil
- 2 cups babyspinach
- 1 cup frozen peas, thawed
- 2 tablespoons vegan parmesan cheese or more to taste

Directions

1. Place a large skillet over medium heat. Add vegetable oil. When oil
2. is heated, add onions and garlic and sauté until the onions are soft.

3. Add pumpkin seeds and ½ cup water and bring to the boil. Simmer for 5-6 minutes. Remove from heat and cool.
4. Transfer into a blender. Add nutritional yeast, milk, basil, thyme, lemon juice, vinegar, flour, salt, pepper and olive oil and blend for 30-40 seconds or until smooth.
5. Pour the blended mixture back into the skillet. Add about ½ cupwater and stir constantly until the sauce thickens. Taste and adjust the seasonings if necessary. Add more water if you find the sauce too thick.
6. Add pasta, spinach, and peas and toss well. Heat thoroughly. 6. Remove from heat. Cover and set aside for a couple of minutes. 7. Garnish with red pepper flakes and vegan

Parmesan cheese andserve.

Cauliflower and Chickpea Stew with Couscous

Ingredients:

- 4 tablespoons olive oil
- 2 heads cauliflower, cut into small florets 2 medium onions, chopped
  10 ounces baby spinach
- 2 cans (15 ounces each) chickpeas, rinsed 2 cans (28 ounces each) whole tomatoes 1 teaspoon ground ginger
- 3 teaspoons ground cumin
- Salt to taste
- Pepper to taste
- 1 cup raisins
- 2 cups couscous
- Hot water, as required

Directions

1. Place a large saucepan over medium heat. Add oil. When oil is heated, add onions and garlic and sauté until the onions are translucent.
2. Add spices and salt and sauté for a few seconds until fragrant.

    Crush the tomatoes and add into the saucepan. Add rest of theingredients except couscous and spinach. Add about 1 cup water. Simmer until cauliflower is tender and the stew thickened.

    Add spinach and cook until it wilts. Remove from heat.
3. Add couscous into a large bowl. Pour about 2 cups of hot waterover it. Cover and set aside for 5-6 minutes. Take a fork and fluff the couscous.

    Serve stew with couscous.

Carrot Lemongrass & Cilantro Soup

Ingredients

- 2 cups vegetable
- ½ red or green chile, diced roughly
- 2 tablespoons soy sauce
- 1 teaspoon sea salt
- Juice of ½ lime
- **For garnish:** Fresh cilantro and sesame seeds
- ½ large brown onion, sliced roughly
- 2 lemongrass sticks, cut in halves
- 3 large carrots, roughly sliced in thick pieces
- 1 large sweet potato, peeled and roughly cut
- 1 large celery stick, roughly cut in 3-4 pieces
- Handful of fresh cilantro (leaves and stems)
- 2 large cloves of garlic
- 1 can of coconut milk

Directions

1. Place all ingredients except for lime juice in the pot and stir through. Lock the lid and make sure the valve is set to Sealing. Press the Manual button and set to High pressure for 7 mins. After 3 beeps, the Instant Pot will start to build up the pressure. Once the timer goes off, allow 5-10 minutes for natural pressure release and then use the quick release method to let off the rest of the steam.
2. Remove the lemongrass piece and transfer the soup's content to a blender or a food processor in 2-3 batches. Puree until smooth and return to another saucepan.
3. Add the lime juice, stir through and taste for salt. You can add more salt or more fish sauce for extra seasoning. Serve with sesame seeds and fresh cilantro over the top.

Instant Pot Achari Aloo

Ingredients

- 1 tsp salt
- ½ tsp red chili powder
- ½ tsp turmeric powder
- 1 tsp dry pomegranate powder
- 2 tsp dried fenugreek leaves
- 1 tbsp mango pickle
- 2 tbsp + 2 tbsp oil
- 5 Potatoes - boiled and cubed
- Whole Spices
- 1 tbsp cumin seeds
- 1 tbsp coriander seeds, pounded
- 5 cloves
- 1 bay leaf
- Dry Spices

Directions

1. Switch Instant Pot on Saute mode, when the pot is hot add 2 tbsp oil.
2. Add whole spices and let them simmer. Now add the dry spices and mix them well.
3. Add the remaining 2 tbsp oil and pickle. Mix this mixture well.
4. Add the potatoes and coat them well with the spice mix.
5. Now close the lid and cancel Saute mode.
6. Select Manual mode and set it for 2 minutes.
7. When time is done , serve the dish hot with paratha or poori.

Stove Top Directions

1. Add oil in the pan, when warm add whole spices.
2. When spices splutter add the dry spices, mix well.
3. Add the pickle and remaining 2 tbsp oil and mix.

4. Add in potatoes and coat them with the prepared spice mix.
5. Cook for 5-8 minutes till potatoes are cooked.

Boiling Potatoes In Instant Pot:

1. Put potatoes in the main pot and cover them with water.
2. Set it at Manual mode for 12 minutes.

Instant Pot Vegan Posole

Ingredients

- 1 tbsp oil (suitable for high temps)
- 2 20 oz cans of jackfruit
- 6 cups vegetable broth
- garnishes 1 14 oz. container of red chile puree (or google how to make your own)
- 2 25 oz. cans hominy
- 1 medium onion
- 8 garlic cloves
-

Directions

1. Set Instant Pot to saute. Add oil, onions, and garlic and saute for 5 minutes.
2. Add red chile puree and continue to cook for a minute.
3. Add jackfruit and cook for 2 more minutes.

4. Use a potato masher to break up the jackfruit and then add 6 cups of broth.
5. Secure lid, set Instant Pot to "Manual" (and "High Pressure") and enter 10 minutes to cook.
6. Allow for natural pressure release (or if you're impatient, wait 20 minutes and then release additional pressure with valve.)
7. Remove lid, add hominy, and set to cook on manual for 1 minute.
8. Allow for natural pressure release (or if you're impatient, wait 20 minutes and then release additional pressure with valve.) Season with salt to taste.
9. Garnishes are completely up to your personal preference but can include lime juice, oregano, red pepper flakes, cilantro, shredded cabbage, and thinly sliced radishes.

Tuscany Style Vegetable Soup

Ingredients:

- Parsley, fresh, for garnish, chopped
- Salt, one half teaspoon
- Tomato paste, two tablespoons
- Tomatoes, two large, diced small
- Vegetable broth, six cups
- Yellow onion, one medium, diced
- Zucchini, one medium, peeled and chopped
- Basil, one tablespoon, finely chopped
- Black pepper, one teaspoon
- Carrot, one-half cup, chopped
- Celery, one-half cup, chopped
- Garlic, four cloves, minced
- Kale, two cups, chopped
- Olive oil, three tablespoons

Directions

1. Fry the onion and the garlic in the heated olive oil in a large soup pot. Then add in the carrots, celery, and the zucchini and cook these for ten minutes while stirring frequently.
2. Mix in the pepper, tomatoes, and salt, stirring to mix well, and cook for two more minutes. Then mix in the vegetable broth and the tomato paste, mix well, and bring the whole mix to a boil.
3. Turn the heat lower and let the mix simmer for fifteen minutes. Put in the parsley and the basil, and then remove the pot from the heat and let the soup sit undisturbed for ten minutes.
4. Garnish with the fresh parsley and serve.

Vegan Tempeh BLT Wrap

Ingredients:

- Cumin, one eighth teaspoon
- Black pepper, one half teaspoon
- Tomato, one half, sliced into two slices
- Avocado, one half, sliced thinly
- Vegan mayo, one tablespoon
- Green leaf lettuce, four large leaves
- Tempeh, one-half packages, sliced thin
- Soy sauce, one and one-half tablespoons
- Maple syrup or agave, one and one half teaspoons
- Olive oil, one tablespoon
- Onion powder, one quarter teaspoon

Directions

1. Blend together in a bowl the syrup, cumin, onion powder, soy sauce, and black pepper in a medium-sized bowl. Mix in the slices of tempeh and let them marinate while you are preparing the other veggies.
2. Wash the leaves of lettuce and dry them with a paper towel. Cut a bit out of the stem part by making a V-shaped cut into it as this will make the lettuce leaves easier to fold. Heat the olive oil over medium heat and add the tempeh slices into the oil. Fry the slices of tempeh for five minutes on each side until they are just a bit blackened on the edges. On a plate lay two lettuce leaves so that they overlap halfway.
3. Lay on the lettuce leaves two slices of the fried tempeh with the vegan mayo, tomatoes, and avocado. Tuck in slightly the ends of the

lettuce leaves and fold them over. Repeat this same process with all of the ingredients.

4. Nutrition info per serving: Calories 382, twenty-six grams fat, twenty-one grams carbs, four grams fiber, five grams sugar, twenty-three grams protein

Millet and Eggplant Chickpea Stew

Ingredients:

- Hot sauce, two tablespoons
- Millet, one cup
- Olive oil, two tablespoons
- Onion, one, diced
- Salt, one half teaspoon
- Tomatoes, one can fourteen ounces, pureed
- Black pepper, one teaspoon
- Chickpeas, one can fourteen ounces, drained
- Cilantro, two tablespoons garnish
- Eggplant, one, cubed
- Garlic, three cloves, minced

Directions

1. Bring the millet to a boil with two cups of water in a medium-sized saucepan over medium heat, then lessen the heat and simmer the millet for twenty-five minutes and then let it cool.
2. While the millet is simmering, you will fry the garlic, onion, and eggplant with the salt and pepper for ten minutes in a large skillet over medium-high heat. Mix in the chickpeas, hot sauce, and tomatoes and cook this mix on low heat for ten minutes. Spoon this mix over the cooked millet in bowls.
3. Nutrition info per serving: Calories 600, fifteen grams fat, one hundred grams carbs, twenty grams protein, seventeen grams sugar

Roasted Vegetables and Lemon Vinaigrette

Ingredients:

- Garlic, two cloves, minced
- Mushrooms, fresh, sliced, one cup
- Olive oil, one tablespoon
- Oregano, fresh chop, one tablespoon
- Parsley, fresh chop, two tablespoons
- Red onion, one, peeled and sliced
- Rosemary, fresh chop, one teaspoon
- Salt, one quarter teaspoon
- Asparagus spears, one pound fresh, trim and cut in two-inch pieces
- Balsamic vinegar, two tablespoons
- Basil, fresh chop, one tablespoon

- Bell pepper, red or green, one cleaned and chopped
- Black olives, ten large, pitted
- Black pepper, one half teaspoon
- Cannellini beans, one fifteen to sixteen-ounce can, drained and rinsed
- Cherry tomatoes, red or yellow, one cup

Directions

1. Heat the oven to 425. Spray oil one eleven by seventeen (or comparable size) baking dishes and set it to the side. Mix rosemary, basil, pepper, salt, oregano, and parsley in a bowl. Use a large bowl to toss together bell pepper, onion, oil, garlic, and mushroom.
2. Mix the bowl of herbs with the bowl of veggies. Pour this mix in the baking dish. Bake the veggies for thirty minutes. Mix the tomatoes, beans, balsamic vinegar, olives, and

asparagus with the roasted vegetables and then sprinkle the veggie mix with the remaining herb mix and combine well. Bake for fifteen more minutes.
3. Nutrition info two cup serving: Calories 360, twelve grams fat, nine grams fiber, twenty-seven grams carbs, forty-three grams protein, six grams sugar

Coffele Fontina Broccoli

Ingredients:

- 1 tsp. black pepper
- 4 Ciabatta rolls
- 4 slices of Fontina cheese
- 1 red onion
- ¼ cup of Dijon mustard
- 1 tsp. salt
- 2 tbsp. coconut oil
- ¼ cup of mayonnaise
- 1 cup of baby spinach
- 2 medium-sized broccolis

Directions

1. Preheat your grill to 400°F (200°C).

2. Cut the broccoli into thick slices or florets. Brush them with olive oil and season with black pepper and salt.
3. Cut the ciabatta rolls in half and lightly brush the cut sides with olive oil. Set them aside.
4. Place the seasoned broccoli slices on the grill and cook them, flipping occasionally, until they become golden brown and slightly charred.
5. Once the broccoli is cooked, top each slice with fontina cheese and allow it to melt.
6. Remove the grilled broccoli steaks from the grill and set them aside. Keep them warm.
7. Place the ciabatta rolls on the grill and cook them for about three minutes, or until they are lightly toasted.
8. In a small bowl, mix together mayonnaise and Dijon mustard. Spread this mixture on the insides of the toasted ciabatta rolls.

9. Assemble the sandwiches by laying the grilled broccoli slices, red onions, and fresh spinach leaves on the bottom bun.
10. Close the sandwiches with the top bun and serve.

Creamy Shallots Le Corti

Ingredients:

- 160g of pasta
- 3-ounces of sliced shallots
- 3-ounces of fresh arugula
- 2 tbsp. nut milk
- 1 tsp. black pepper
- 3 cloves of garlic
- 4-ounces of cottage cheese
- 4 tbsp. fresh parsley
- 1 tsp. salt
- 1 tsp. nutmeg

Directions

1. Cook the pasta according to the package Directionsuntil it is al dente. Drain and set aside.
2. In a large skillet, heat some olive oil over medium heat. Add the minced garlic and sliced shallots to the skillet. Cook until they become soft and fragrant.
3. Add the chopped parsley and arugula to the skillet. Cook for a few minutes until the arugula wilts.
4. Reduce the heat to low. Add the cottage cheese to the skillet and stir well to combine with the other ingredients. Allow it to heat through and become creamy.
5. Pour in the nut milk gradually, stirring continuously until you achieve the desired creamy consistency. The amount of nut milk needed may vary, so add it gradually to avoid making the sauce too thin.

6. Season the sauce with salt, pepper, and ground nutmeg to taste. Adjust the seasonings according to your preference.
7. Add the drained pasta to the skillet and toss gently to coat the pasta with the creamy shallot sauce.
8. Serve the Creamy Shallots Le Corti immediately, while it's still warm.

Greek Atma Pizzas

Ingredients:

- 1 tsp. basil
- 1 large jalapeno pepper
- 2 broccolis
- 2 tomatoes
- 1/4 cup of tomato sauce
- 1 tsp. red pepper flakes

Directions

1. Preheat the oven to 350°F (175°C) to ensure it is adequately heated for baking the pizza.
2. Slice the bell pepper into thin strips and arrange them on a baking sheet. This will add a vibrant and flavorful topping to the pizza.
3. Sprinkle the desired amount of cheese over the sliced bell pepper. Feta cheese or mozzarella are common choices for Greek-

style pizzas, but you can use any cheese you prefer.

4. Spoon tomato sauce over the cheese and spread it evenly. The tomato sauce serves as the base for the pizza and adds a rich and tangy flavor.
5. Scatter the broccoli florets and halved cherry tomatoes on top of the cheese and sauce. These ingredients provide freshness, texture, and additional nutrients to the pizza.
6. Place the baking sheet with the prepared pizza in the preheated oven. Bake for approximately 10 minutes, or until the cheese is melted and bubbly, and the crust is golden brown. Cooking times may vary, so keep an eye on the pizza to prevent it from overcooking.
7. Remove the pizza from the oven when it is done, and sprinkle fresh basil leaves over the top. The basil leaves add a fragrant and

aromatic element to the pizza, enhancing its overall flavor.

Zucchini Fritters

Ingredients:

- ½ Teaspoon of cumin seeds
- ½ Teaspoon of coriander seeds
- ½ Teaspoon of black ground pepper
- ¼ Teaspoon of ground cinnamon
- ¼ Teaspoon of ground cardamom
- ½ Teaspoon of salt
- 1 Tablespoon of chia seed
- ¼ Cup of oat flour
- 2 Tablespoon of breadcrumbs
- 1 Small of shredded zucchini
- ½ Cup of chopped carrots
- 3 Minced garlic cloves

- ½ inch of grated ginger
- 1 cayenne
- 1 and ½ cups of cooked and drained chickpeas
    - Oil

Directions:

1. Shred the zucchini and add it to a small and deep bowl with a processor.
2. Press your zucchini into a paper towel and process the carrots, the ginger and the chilli with the help of a food processor and add it to a bowl
3. Process the chickpeas until it become coarsely blended
4. Make the mixture of spices
5. Crush the coriander and the cumin with the black pepper with a mortar pestle.
6. Heat around ½ teaspoon of oil in a small skillet and when it becomes hot, add your

crushed spices and cook it until it becomes fragrant.
7. Add your spices to your bowl and add the cinnamon, the cardamom, the salt, the flour, the flaxseed and combine it well.
8. Add the flour and mix it in. Add the breadcrumbs.
9. Form the patties and cook it with oil in a large skillet over a medium heat for around 5 minutes on each side.
10. Bake it at about at 400° F degrees for about 25 minutes
11. Serve and enjoy your ketchup.

Oven Roasted Chickpeas

Ingredients:

- 2 Cups of canned chickpeas
- 3 Cups of white vinegar
- 1 Teaspoon of Coarse sea salt
- 2 Teaspoons of extra virgin olive oil

Directions:

1. Line a baking sheet with a tin foil or a parchment paper.
2. Take the chickpeas and the vinegar and place it into a medium pan.
3. Add 1 pinch of sea salt and let the chickpeas boil for around 30 minutes
4. Preheat your oven to about 400° F. Meanwhile, drain your chickpeas and place it on the line baking sheet; then drizzle with a little bit of olive oil

5. Add the sea salt and mix with your fingers
6. Roast the chickpeas for 35 minutes and make sure to flip it after halfway.
7. Serve and enjoy your chickpeas!

Banana Bread

Ingredients:

- 1 Teaspoon of baking soda
- 1 Teaspoon of salt
- 1 Teaspoon of cinnamon
- 1 tablespoon of chopped walnuts
- 2 Medium ripe bananas
- 1 Peeled and diced apple
- ½ Cup of sugar
- 1 and ¾ cups of whole-wheat flour
- ½ Cup of applesauce

Directions:

1. Preheat your oven to about 350°F. Grease a medium loaf pan with vegetable oil
2. In a medium bowl, mash your bananas with a fork.

3. Add the sugar, the diced apple, the flour, the applesauce, the baking soda, the salt, and the cinnamon to your bowl, and mix it very well.
4. Pour your ingredients to your prepared greased pan; then sprinkle with the chopped walnuts
5. Bake for about 50 minutes
6. Remove the bread from the oven and set it aside for around 15 minutes
7. Serve and enjoy your bread!

www.ingramcontent.com/pod-product-compliance
Lightning Source LLC
La Vergne TN
LVHW020436070526
838199LV00063B/4759